THE WORD OF GOD ABOVE ALL THINGS WILL WORK FOR YOU

BY

Dr. Roger R. Hagwood

Copyright © 2004 by Dr. Roger R. Hagwood

Published in Lanham, Maryland,
by Pneuma Life Publishing

The Word of God Will Work For You Above All Things
by Dr. Roger R. Hagwood

Printed in the United States of America

ISBN 1-594676-29-1

All rights reserved solely by the author. The author guarantees all contents are original and do not infringe upon the legal rights of any other person or work. No part of this book may be reproduced in any form without the permission of the author. The views expressed in this book are not necessarily those of the publisher.

Scripture quotations noted NKJV are from the New King James Version of the Bible. Copyright © 1979, 1980, 1982, 1990. Thomas Nelson, Inc., Publishers.

Scripture quotations noted KJV are from the King James Version of the Holy Bible.

www.xulonpress.com

CONTENTS

Acknowledgements		vii
Introduction		ix
Chapter 1	Transferred Spiritual Strength	11
	Hearing and Seeing the Word of God	12
Chapter 2	The Word of God Performs Over All External Forces	15
Chapter 3	The Word Contains Life and Spirit	19
Chapter 4	The Word Produces Life	23
Chapter 5	God Picked Up the Check Over Two Thousand Years Ago Through Jesus Christ	27
Chapter 6	Receive From God	29
Chapter 7	An Unction to Function	33
Chapter 8	Remembering God	37
Chapter 9	Revelation of God	39
Chapter 10	Testimony	41
Chapter 11	God Answers Sinner's Prayer	45
Chapter 12	Commissioned Things	49
Chapter 13	With Him	51

Chapter 14	Above All Things Divine Release	53
Chapter 15	God's Presence	55
Chapter 16	Get Acquainted With God	59
Chapter 17	Reserved Released Power	61
Chapter 18	All Things Are Possible	65
Chapter 19	Blessed	69
Chapter 20	Offensive Against Darkness	73
Chapter 21	Propelled	75
Chapter 22	A Fire Influenced Destiny	77
Chapter 23	The Kingdom of God Seizes Darkness	79
Chapter 24	Too Equipped to Get Whipped	81
Chapter 25	Relevant Leaders	83
Chapter 26	Rich Above All Things	87

ACKNOWLEDGEMENTS

A special thank you to my lovely wife Sandra G. Hagwood. Another thank you goes to my deceased grandmother, Ms. Daisy Hagwood, who imparted the spirit of prayer into me.

Thanks to Mrs. Valaire Pilson, who is married to my brother-in-law Mr. Robert Pilson, who labored intensely to make this book a vital effective resource. Always, thank you to First Christian Church, Stuart, Virginia's congregation which taught me to propel above all things in pursuit of the truth.

Finally, thanks to my parents, Nathaniel and Mable Hagwood, Sr., who instilled positive and enriched values in all their children. They are constantly reinforcing those values. During the process of this book Mr. Nathaniel Hagwood went to be with the Lord on May 19, 2000, and he is greatly missed by his entire family. To God be the Glory!

INTRODUCTION

This book's content is a deposit into the lives of men, women, boys, and girl's whose interest is godly. The word of God contains the substance, power, and strength that is needed for the twenty first century. This book is one of those resources that will help prepare leaders in the twenty first century. The word of God will resolve issues above all things. God's word will heighten and strengthen your walk with God. Readers will develop a deeper relationship with God. The anointing will radiate lives and enhance their expectations from God above all things.

CHAPTER 1

Transferred Spiritual Strength

And suddenly there came a sound from heaven, as of a rushing mighty wind and it filled the whole house where they were sitting **(Acts 2:2)**. Jesus preformed a mighty work on the Day of Pentecost. Suddenly, Jesus transferred his spiritual strength, power, and authority to believers who would stand against well established traditions of men.

Jesus said to them, "All too well you reject the commandment of God, that you may keep your tradition." Making the word of God of no effect through your traditions, which you have handed down, and many such things you do **(Mark 7:9-13)**.

Instead of believing God, people are deeply rooted in traditions, denominations, and beliefs. The Holy Ghost had to come to break down ungodly traditions and other ungodly things and remove them from lives of believer's.

The Holy Ghost will erase every ungodly thing from your life and then replace it with the life found in Jesus. The Holy Ghost is active now in the world. He will not leave until He presents the kingdom of God to the King.

We need to hear the Holy Spirit's voice and see Him moving among mankind while He is still on the earth. How can we hear and see the Holy Ghost? The only way is to hear and see the word of God. This example explains how.

Hearing and Seeing the Word of God

Luke states, "and He answered and said unto them, 'my mother and brethren are these, which hear the word of God, and do it.' Now it came to pass on a certain day, that he went into a ship with His disciples: And He said unto them **Let us go over unto the other side of the lake.**

And they launched forth. But as they sailed He fell asleep: And there came down a storm of wind on the lake: And they were filled with water and were in Jeopardy. And they came to wake Him, and awoke Him, saying 'Master, Master, we perish.' Then He arose and rebuked the wind and the raging of the water. And they ceased and were calm. And he said unto them, 'where is your Faith?' And they being afraid wondered, saying, one to another, 'what Manner of Man is this! For he commandeth even the winds and water, and they obey him' " (**Luke 8:21-25**).

"Now faith is the substance of **things** hoped for, the evidence of things not seen" (Hebrews 11:1, emphasis added). "All **things** were made by Him: and without him was not anything made that was made" (John 1:3, emphasis added). "And God saw every **thing** that he had made, and, behold, it was very good. And the evening and the morning were the sixth day" **(Genesis 1:31).**

In Genesis, God **said** and **saw**, We must hear what is said before we can **see** the results. "So then faith cometh by hearing, and hearing by the Word of God" **(Romans 10:17).** We need to hear the Word of God, just as Jesus told the disciples to hear the Word of God.

Today, we also need to see the Word of God in action. Prior to the disciples leaving for the other side, Jesus spoke these words. "**Let us go over unto the other side of the lake.**"

The Spoken Word "**Let us go over unto the other side of the Lake**" was strength and power enough to get the Disciples to the other side of the lake. Satan tried to stop Jesus and the disciples from the other side of the lake. Legion a (Demonic) influenced man was on the other side. The demons knew that Jesus would free the demonic man. Jesus is the word of God that is settled in heaven to loose things in the earth. There will always be opposition to your blessings, but the word of God will bring you through into a blessed place.

CHAPTER 2

The Word of God Performs Over All External Forces

⋆⇌⇋⋆

"Forever, O Lord your word is settled in heaven. Your faithfulness endures to all generations: You established the earth, and it abides," **(Psalms 119:89-90)**.

We have confidence in what God has said about us because His word is settled in heaven. Jesus Christ, who has covered us with His blood and righteousness, is sitting at the right hand of the Father. He sent the Holy Ghost to lead and guide us into all truths. Now, all of heaven is supporting us, because as believers we have power, dominion, and authority over all external forces. His power towards us who believe, according to the working of His mighty power which He worked in Christ when He raised Him from the dead and seated Him at His right Hand in heavenly places far above all principalities and power and might and dominion, and every name that is named not only in this age, but also in that which is to come. And He put all things under His feet, and gave Him to be head over all things to the Church.

"Now unto Him who is able to do exceedingly abundantly above all that we ask or think, according to the power that works in us, to Him be glory in the Church by Christ Jesus to all generations, forever and ever. Amen," **(Ephesians 3:20-21)**.

Above all appears again and again in the scriptures. **Above all** makes us cognizant of the fact that everything is already worked out **above All things. Above all** that we ask or think. First, we have to ask and think according to the Holy Ghost Power that works in us.

Whatever we are asking or thinking is important to the almighty God.

He's saying, "That's good, but I can do better than what you are asking or thinking." The great I AM will do exceedingly abundantly **above all** that we ask or think. He is working in us while His exceeding abundant supply is manifesting in the natural realm.

The Holy Ghost strengthens us to take ownership in the spiritual realm until it appears in the natural realm. What are believers possessing?

1. We appropriate God's Word.
2. We learn how to say what God says about our circumstances.

Meanwhile, some people will say you are lying when they don't see any manifestation. Believers are not lying when they say what God said in His Holy Word. Therefore, we have a right and a privilege to say what He says about us.

His Word says, "Beloved, I wish **above all things** that you prosper and be in good health, even as your soul prospers" **(3 John 1:2, NKJV)**. Also, we say it **above all** things because John stated, "Jesus said to him, I am the way, the truth, and life. No one comes to the Father except through me." **(John 14:6).** The truth is to be believed **above all** things. **Above all** things this Gospel truth stands because it is His Word. His Word is life and spirit. It's okay to speak what God's life and Spirit says about all things. Whatever you and almighty God say together will never stop. That's how powerful His Word is today. He spoke light into existence and it never stopped. We have one of the greatest blessings ever bestowed upon us as believers and that blessing is His Word.

CHAPTER 3

The Word Contains Life and Spirit

The Word is full of the creative energy of the almighty God. There is a current of creative energy flowing out of your mouth when His word is used **above all things.**

1. The divine nature of God is in His Word as you speak.
2. His supernatural strength is in His Word.
3. His performance is activated into whatever situation the Word is spoken
4. His authority is in the Word.
5. His excellency is in the Word.
6. He is committed to His Word.

"In the beginning was the Word, and the Word was with God, and the Word was God. He was in the beginning with God. **All things** were made through him, and without Him nothing was made that was made," (**John 1:1-3, emphasis added**). Almighty God's spoken Word makes Him the Author of all things. Therefore, **all things** have to obey the Creator's voice. Now we see why it is necessary to speak God's Word instead of ours. At His Word, all things move and obey.

God's Word made things in the universe. The Word of Almighty God can make things in our life because His Word is immutable.

"Thus God, determining to show more abundantly to the heirs of promise the immutability of His counsel, confirmed it by an oath, that by two immutable things, in which it is impossible for God to lie, we might have strong consolation, who have fled for refuge to lay hold of the Hope set before us"(**Hebrews 6:17-18 NKJV**).

Heirs of promise are assured of God's sovereignty over all things. God doesn't speak without success (**Isaiah 45:19**).

"I have sworn by myself, the word is gone out of my mouth in righteousness, and shall not return, that unto me every knee shall bow, every tongue shall confess,"(**Isaiah 45:23**).

Remember the former **things** of old: For I am God, and there is none else, I am God and there is none like me. Declaring the end from the beginning, and from ancient times the **things** that are not yet done, saying my counsel shall stand, and I will do all my pleasure. (**Isaiah 9-10**).

"Calling a ravenous bird from the east, the man that executed my counsel from a far Country: **yea I have spoken it,** I will also bring it to pass, I have purposed it. I will also do it. Hearken unto me, ye stout hearted, that are far from righteousness," **(Isaiah 46:11-12, emphasis added)**.

See, hear, and use the Word of God until you tap into the real power of God in your life.

We are in the real power of God because the Word contains the master elements to create things.

CHAPTER 4

The Word Produces Life

"If ye abide in me, and my words abide in you, you will ask what you desire, and it shall be done for you. By this my father is glorified that you bear much fruit: so you will be my disciples," **(John 15:7-8)**.

The key is to abide in the Word, and God's Word must abide in us. The word is the life producer and is powerful enough to produce life under any circumstance. Once spoken, it stands alone.

The word existed before the creation of man. The Word is one of our best tools, but for centuries we have over looked it. Now, many believers who are expounding upon and obeying the Word of God are growing by leaps and bounds. Believers who reside in the presence of the Almighty will produce life because in His presence is life.

And He said to me, Son of man, can these bones live? So I answered, 'O Lord God, you know.' Again He said to me, Prophesy to these bones, and say to them 'O dry bones, hear the Word of the

Lord' "(**Ezekiel 37:3-4**).

God's word will produce life in any dry situation. Meanwhile, we must hear the Word spoken to our poverty, sickness, and obscurity. Also He said to me, "Prophesy to the breath, prophesy, son of Man, and say to the breath, Thus says the Lord God." (**Ezekiel 37:9**)

Come from the four winds, O breath, and breathe on these slain, that they may live. (**Ezekiel 37:9**)

God command us to live through Jesus Christ—His Word made flesh. The word manifests God's spirit in action. Upon contact with our spirit, God's word quickens, strengthens, forms, produces, and reproduces His character and attributes. There is so much uninterrupted power in God's word that flows until God changes or moves, whatever is in His path.

"God said, and I will put enmity between you and the woman, and between your seed and her seed. He shall bruise your head and you should bruise His heel" (**Genesis 3:15**).

The enemy has been killing the first born from the beginning of time trying to stop God's Man servant—Jesus Christ—who has already bruised his head. By the power of His blood, Jesus Christ stopped Satan in his tracks. The blood of Jesus is the most powerful thing in the spirit realm to break strongholds.

"Behold, I stand at the door and knock, if anyone hears my voice and opens the door, I will come in to him and dine with him, and he with me. To him who overcomes I will grant to sit with me on my throne, as I also overcame and sat down with my father on

His throne. He who has an ear, let him hear what the spirit says to the churches" (**Revelation 3:20-22**).

Jesus is knocking at the door of sin, poverty, sickness, disease, despair, loneliness, and other problems. Invite Jesus in. The amazing thing about Jesus, nothing is impossible with Him. He will make a way right into your problems and circumstances to remove them. That's the uniqueness of Jesus. He doesn't need a right way, denominational way, or a religious way. Wherever there are problems, He is the Way because Jesus's grace is sufficient.

People are praying, but not receiving.

"Therefore I say to you, whatever things you ask, when you pray, **believe that you receive them,** and you will have them." **(Mark 11:24)**

This is where the body of Christ has missed it. Today, we have some sincere; Holy Ghost-filled Christians who are asking, but not receiving what God has for them.

We must receive the blessings in the Spirit realm before things manifest themselves. When a person goes to the store, he first picks out the items, buys them, and then have the items delivered. They are his now, even though they are not in the person's house. Even though a person confesses having a new chair, sofa, table, lamp, and stove, they are not delivered yet, but they are his.

Everything you ever prayed for is yours. Receive it, and thank God for paying for your things **above all other things.** It's yours! It's yours! Thank God Almighty, it's mine too. It's good to be on the receiving end. There is one slight problem. I don't have room enough to receive all of this stuff God has for me because His Word states, "Bring all the tithes into the storehouse that there may be food in my house, and try me now in this, says the Lord of hosts, if I will not open for you the windows of heaven and pour out for you such blessing that there will not be room enough to receive it" **(Malachi 3:10)**.

We can't receive it all, therefore, We will have to share with others. We will want to give it away, but I can't keep up with God's giving; He is too awesome. Meanwhile, I receive now, everything. We appreciate the ministering angels who are there for the heirs of salvation.

"Are they not all ministering spirits sent forth to minister for those who will inherit salvation?" **(Hebrews 1:14)**

CHAPTER 5

God Picked Up the Check Over Two Thousand Years Ago Through Jesus Christ

Therefore he says; when He ascended on high, He led captivity captive and gave gifts to men. (Now this, "He ascended." What does it mean but that He also first descended into the lower parts of the earth? He who descended is also the one who ascended for above all the heavens, that He might fill all things **(Ephesians 4:8-10)**.

Jesus went to hell and severed Satan's grip upon the church because He had already redeemed us through His blood. Christ made a show of His power openly. I prefer to call this divine release by Christ. Divine release began in the Old Testament. He divinely released Sarah's womb. Second, He divinely released Lot from Sodom and Gomorrah. Next, the children of Israel crossed the Red Sea. In the New Testament divine release took place when Lazarus was resurrected from the grave. Another release was when Peter was freed from jail. Paul and Silas were also freed from jail.

The spirit of divine release is active today in believers because, we who were dead in our trespasses and sins have been made alive with Christ.

"Even when we were dead in trespasses, made us alive together with Christ (by grace you have been saved)" **(Ephesians 2:5)**.

The spirit of divine release put us in the body of Jesus—the church. We are in unity with Jesus Christ the anointed One. Therefore, when we command something to be released in Jesus' name, it is released by His power that works in us.

We have transcended time, problems, situations, sickness, poverty, and any other thing. The body of Christ is one with Jesus **far above all of these things.**

"Therefore I say unto you, whatever things you ask when you pray, believe that you receive them and you will have them" **(Mark 11:24)**.

CHAPTER 6

Receive From God

Therefore my prayer is:

1. Thank God for a Holy Ghost-fire-filled church.
2. Thank God for a faithful church.
3. Thank God for a healed and delivered church.
4. Thank God for a giving church.
5. Thank God for a growing church.
6. Thank God for a witnessing church.
7. Thank God for a praying church.
8. Thank God for a triumphant church.
9. Thank God for an anointed church.
10. Thank God for a victorious church.

Thank God We received all the above for our church. This reminds us of a photo of blessings and a instant snap shot. You take the picture now, and then it is developed instantly. That's God's word in inception. It develops out of the Spirit realm into the natural realm. Just like your instant camera. God's manifestation is real in the Spirit realm and the natural realm because He made all things.

Christ has the power to push out our prayer request after we receive it in the spirit realm. Stop claiming and receive or accept in the spirit realm, so that thing you have been praying for will manifest. Then, you can move on to the next thing. Remember things have to obey the Word of God.

Receive from God and stop claiming what is already yours. It was yours before you set foot on this earth. God put your stuff in lay-away for you. Believers, receive your stuff please. It's time for the church to have what God says we have. It is ours. Stop begging, looking, and feeling, and receive your inheritance from almighty God in the name of Jesus.

The Lord had me to pray this prayer for First Christian Church in Stuart, Virginia.

Therefore, I prayed, do not cease to give thanks for you, making mention of you in my prayers. That the God of our Lord Jesus Christ, the Father of Glory, may give to you the spirit of wisdom and revelation in the knowledge of Him the eyes of your understanding being enlightened, that you may know what is the hope of His calling, what are the riches of the glory of His inheritance in the saints, and what is the exceeding greatness of His power toward us who believe, according to the working of His mighty power. Which He worked in Christ when He raised Him from the dead and seated Him at His right hand in the heavenly places, far above all principality and power and might and dominion, and every name that is named, not only in this age but also in that which is to come.

"And he put all things under His feet, and gave Him to be head over all things to the church, which is His body, the fullness of Him who fills all in all" **(Ephesians 1:16-23)**.

"For this reason I bow my knees to the Father of our Lord Jesus Christ, from whom the whole family in heaven and earth is named, that He would grant you, according to the riches of His glory, to be strengthened with might through His spirit in the inner man, that Christ may dwell in your hearts through faith. That you, being rooted and grounded in love, may be able to comprehend with all saints what is the width and length and depth and height to know the love of Christ, which passes knowledge, that you may be filled with all the fullness of God. Now unto Him who is able to do exceedingly abundantly above all that we ask or think, according to the power that works in us to Him be glory in the church by Christ Jesus to all generations, forever and ever. Amen" **(Ephesians 3:14-21)**.

Now, the church is blooming. People are returning to the faith. The church did a 360-degree turn once it received what Christ had already done and said thanks to Christ. The Spirit of the true and living almighty God had the church to thank Him for saving, healing, delivering, and baptizing them in Holy Ghost fire. The results are overwhelming because God showed up! Glory to almighty God in the name of Jesus Christ.

The key to any successful Christian will be to hold on to God in the face of adverse circumstances. Also, each individual must get to know God for himself.

The woman at the well met another man. She was already familiar with men. Meanwhile, she met a better man who could satisfy all her needs. The man she met was Jesus. This was published throughout the town **(see John 4:29)**. The woman then left her water pot went her way into the city, and said to the men, come, see a man who told me all things that I ever did could this be the Christ? Then they went out of the city and came to Him (**John 4:28-30**).

People are coming to this man Jesus all over the world now. His impact is greater today than ever before.

Millions of people throughout the world are turning to Christ because they are realizing that they need something greater than what they are experiencing. The woman left her water and pot for the true and living water (Jesus). Her excitement caused men to seek Him rather than seeking her.

CHAPTER 7

An Unction to Function

Over and over we see people seeking Jesus **above all things.** **Above all things** we need, an unction to function. Jesus gives us that unction through His true and living Word. This unction is the anointing.

The unction is not based on feelings, chill bumps, or sensations, thoughts, opinions, religious doctrines, or attitudes. An anointing is an unction to function in the face of unpopular opinion. This unction will raise you above any paralyzing situation because of a dependency upon the word of God.

It's time for all believers to square their shoulders in the face of opposition by moving into enemy territory with an unction to function. The unction to function is "I can do all things through Christ (anointed one), which strengtheneth me" **(Phil. 4:13).** Therefore, we know who has already done the work but we have to accept it by functioning in the anointing.

The anointing gives believers continuous strength that is not of this world. Supernatural strength from the Holy Ghost that is forever present here in the earth. Jesus is rushing grace, favor, anointing, might and power everyday to His people. He rushed this strength to us on the day of Pentecost. Therefore, we have no excuse for not functioning in the anointing by faith.

"Now faith is the substance of things hoped for and the evidence of things not seen" **(Hebrews 11:1)**. Faith is now in our lives and receiving the Holy Ghost's help is now. It's so simple to accept by saying "thank You, Jesus."

The Bible states" in His presence is fullness of joy" **(Psalms 16:11)**. When we go to the grocery store there is all kind of food. We can get what we need while we are there to satisfy our thirst or hunger. It is the same way in the presence of God. We can satisfy our hunger and thirst after righteousness. Because the anointing is a gift, we can walk out of churches throughout the world satisfied if we would accept the truth.

"And you shall know the truth and the truth will make you free" **(John 8:36)**.

"For the Lord is good and His mercy is everlasting and His truth endureth to all generations" **(Psalms 100:5)**.

We have everlasting strength, power, purpose, provisions, and His presence to carry us through any situation. That's why it is necessary to know the Almighty God personally.

A personal intimate relationship is essential to excellence. He moves when you move. The Holy Ghost is our helper or partner. We move together to confirm God's word. He is His word in action on behalf of His children. That's why the psalmist stated, "Bless the Lord, O my soul and all that is in me" **(Psalms 103:1)**. The anointing is in us because greater is He that is in me than He that is in the world. **(John 4:48)**.

A great anointing lives in us in the presence of the Holy Ghost. He is the resurrection Spirit with all power. Therefore, all power resides in and about us at all times. That's why we must have an unction to function. This unction is greater than singing, shouting, dancing, playing instruments, or any position. An unction that excels human knowledge wisdom and skills.

However, this unction will enhance your singing, shouting, dancing, and playing instruments, and positions to greatness. "But you have an anointing from the Holy one and you know all things" **(John 2:20)**. "But the anointing which you have received from Him abides in you, and you do not need anyone to teach you, but as the same anointing teaches you concerning all things and is true, and is not a lie, and just as it has taught you, you will abide in him." **(John 2:21)**

First, we have to recognize the anointing by knowing who He is in the Spirit. Next, it is necessary to receive the anointing. Also, we know that He comes from God. The anointing is here to perform in our lives to destroy yokes and remove burdens.

"It shall come to pass in that day, that his burden will be taken away from your shoulders, and his yoke from your neck, and the yoke will be destroyed because of the anointing" **(Isaiah 10:27)**.

That day is here now! "For He says, "In an acceptable time I have heard you and in the day of salvation I have helped you." Behold now is the accepted time; behold, now is the day of salvation" **(2 Corinthians 6:2)**. Prophets prophesied this day unto us. The acceptable year of the Lord is here today. The acceptable year means divine release.

Divine release is taking place throughout the body of Christ. People are receiving, healing, deliverance, joy, prosperity, and soundness everywhere in the body of Christ. The Lord spoke to me about receiving when I read about Him raising Lazarus. He told me to thank Him and receive. Now, I am receiving from God in a mighty way. To God be all the glory and honor!

CHAPTER 8

Remembering God

"And you shall remember the Lord your God, for it is He who gives you power to get wealth, that He may establish His covenant which He swore to your fathers, as it is this day" **(Deuteronomy 8:18)**.

God is sharing His wealth with the body of Christ. I call it His wealth because He gives us power to get it. He is fulfilling His covenant when we become wealthy.

"Wealth and riches shall be in your house and His righteousness endures forever" **(Psalms 112:3)**. It is right for Him to give you wealth and riches. The blessings of the Lord make one rich, and He adds no sorrow with it **(Proverbs 10:22)**. It is God's desire to bless you and not add any sorrow with it. Remember God in all you endeavors.

CHAPTER 9

Revelation of God

The greatest revelation of all believers is when we discover that we are redeemed from the curse of the law. The first Adam, the original man, sinned and broke relations with God. The second Adam, Jesus, redeemed us from the curse by putting us back into relationship and fellowship with our Father. It's good to know that we are operating in an offensive posture and not a defensive one.

In retrospect, I was busy trying to obtain knowledge through schooling. There is nothing wrong with preparing yourself. Also, I was running here and there trying to impress other ministers or get into their good graces. Another thing, I was trying to fill every office I could obtain. Then I woke up one day and realized, "seek ye first the kingdom of God and **His righteousness,** and **all** these **things** shall be added unto you" **(Matthew 6:33, emphasis added).** I had to see the right one **above all things** to get **things.**

CHAPTER 10

Testimony

I grew up in Maybeury, West Virginia, attending Maybeury Elementary School where Ms. Doubty and Ms. Poole planted an educational and spiritual foundation in me. We had prayer and Bible verses every morning. This was a red brick school that was between a railroad track and a creek. There, I made good grades, but I stayed sick with asthma. I remember my grandmother standing with the door open at night for me to get my breath. However, God healed me. Next, I attended Elkhorn High School where I graduated with a high school diploma.

Meanwhile, my face and head would go numb while I was in high school. I never told my parents or my grandparents. I would pray every night asking God to remove the numbness from my face until he did. I was sincere when I prayed. He heard me and healed me. To God be all the glory! After graduating from high school, I moved to New York. Disappointed, I went into the United States

Army in 1964. From there I went to Korea, Vietnam, and Japan. I was wounded in Vietnam in Tayninh Providence on September 15, 1966, while on a search and destroy mission, But God's grace saved me because the enemy was aiming for my heart, but he hit my right elbow.

Then, I was sent to Japan where I stayed in the hospital several months paralyzed in my right arm from nerve damage. Again, God showed up giving me usage of my right arm. I thank God for great doctors, nurses, and physical therapists. God is awesome. I returned home in 1967 where I met Ms. Sandra Pilson who later became Mrs. Sandra Hagwood. Later, we had Edward, Keisha, Daniele, and Samonte', respectively.

My salvation didn't come until I was thirty years old. I knew about God, but I didn't have a relationship with God. However, when I said yes to God's will, I committed myself to God, not a religion, denomination, tradition, or church. I made the commitment to the almighty God through the Word of God. God has taught me through the Holy Ghost that He is the Author and Finisher of my faith. God's Word has truly enlightened me by watching Him perform His Word through Jesus Christ. I am thrilled to be one of His student's because "it is He that hath made us and not we ourselves" **(Psalms 100:3)**.

Once I began to learn that I need God all the time, it transformed my life. God is so awesome; I can't describe how great He is. He was the best thing that ever happened to me. God will train you in the things of the spirit if you desire to know them and Him.

"God is a Spirit and they that worship Him must worship Him in spirit and truth" **(John 4:24).**

CHAPTER 11

God Answers Sinners' Prayers

God answered my prayers to heal me and save me. There is controversy surrounding the following scripture. "They brought him who formerly was blind to the Pharisees" **(John 9:13)**. Now we know that God does not hear sinners; but if anyone is a worshipper of God and does his will, He hears him **(John 9:31)**.

The Pharisees also called Jesus a sinner. That's where religion obtained this from in churches. Remember, the Pharisees were religious. The previous statements have kept many people from seeking God because they are saying God will not hear me (a sinner). "Then all the tax collector's and the sinner's drew near to Him to hear Him. And the Pharisees and scribes complained, saying, this man receives sinners and eats with them" **(Luke 15:1-2)**.

Jesus Christ's anointing draws sinners. However, we always find religious folks complaining about their doctrines or religious affiliations as the Pharisees. Yes, Jesus hears sinner's prayers and He receives them unto Himself. "I say unto you that likewise there will be more joy in heaven over one sinner who repents than over ninety-nine just persons who need no repentance" **(Luke 15:7)**.

Make a joyful noise unto the Lord all ye lands. Serve the Lord with gladness; come before His presence with singing. Know that the Lord, He is God. It is He that has made us and not we ourselves. We are His people and the sheep of His pasture. Enter into His gates with thanksgiving and into His courts with praise. Be thankful unto Him and Bless His name. For the Lord is good and His mercy is everlasting, and His truth endures to all generations" **(Psalm 100)**.

Truth is being magnified from coast to coast, from country to country, and kingdom to kingdom. Churches are lifting up the truth and it's settling in the hearts of believers all over the world. The truth settling in the hearts of men, women, boys, and girls causing them to **believe and receive above all things.** "Beloved, I wish **above all things,** that thou mayest prosper and be in health even as [thy] soul prospers" **(3 John 3:2), emphasis added)**. Absorb "above all things" into your spirit because it's one of the keys to your breakthrough. It has been my breakthrough along with other scriptures. I have discovered saying what Jesus says about me is more important than anything in heaven and earth.

Loose Jesus' words into your life today. Whatever is loosed on earth is loosed in heaven. Heaven and earth agree to manifest whatever you loosed in the spirit realm.

Jesus said these words, and I say what my elder brother and daddy said. Daddy said it, and I believe it. I can remember when I was a child I was glad to say what daddy said because I believed what he said. Now, my heavenly Father is saying these things to me and **you above all things.** Why don't you believe and receive with me? This is one of the greatest deposits the body of Christ has ever received. Notice I say one of the greatest, because other people have been used by Christ to make a deposit into the body of Christ. So, here is one of my contributions to the body of Christ. It's rich in content because the anointing is in the deposit by Christ through me.

Christ is the central theme in this book **above all things.** Understanding how Christ gives to the body, Christ is everyone's quest in life. Life becomes more fulfilling once individuals learn how to function in the anointing through Christ. First seek ye the kingdom of God and His righteousness and all these things will be added.

Notice Christ's deposit adds. We need to notice **added** because Christ is about addition and multiplication. I don't see Christ taking away from people. Meanwhile, the Bible states, "the thief came to steal kill and destroy, but I came that you might have life and that more abundantly" **(John 10:10)**, notice Christ is into abundance. I call abundance multiplication or more than enough. More than enough is only learned and understood through seeking Christ in spirit and truth.

Again, one most lift himself above **all things** through the anointed words of Christ to find Christ first and then things. Remember Christ first, then things **above all things**. We have to ascend to the word of God. The word descended once but it ascended to the Father. The word ascends us through the anointing.

That is the Holy Spirit who gives us the unction to function **<u>above all things.</u>** The strength and power in the Holy Spirit amazes all believers. I can't see Him, but I trust Him with my life. He is my life forever.

That's why David stated, "Bless the Lord, O my soul and all that is within me, bless His Holy Name! Bless the Lord, O my soul, and forget, not all His benefits" **(Psalm 103:1-2)**. I didn't understand this division of Psalm early on in my Christian life. But one morning the Lord woke me up, speaking these words into my soul. Then, I discovered what they meant. David had killed people, committed adultery, but he discovered the nature of God. David realized that after he repented of his sins, he was free because the almighty God had pardoned him. Next, he realizes newness in him from God.

Now, we have Jesus Christ, His blood and righteousness given to us if we accept it. I began to think about how free we are in Jesus Christ. Then, I thought about the rights and privileges we have as heirs and joint-heirs with Christ.

CHAPTER 12

Commissioned Things

Then I commissioned some things in my life above all things because Jesus' word is final. He is the Word made flesh. Not only can the word be made flesh, but also the word can produce all things. Thank God for the Word of God. Meanwhile, we don't have to beat people up and throw stones across our pulpits. It is a waste of time and money. Nor do we need to spend time and money scandalizing politicians, denominations, and races. We need to present Jesus Christ (The anointed one) as good news. Let the anointing activate the divine nature of Christ in the lost.

"When the spirit of truth has come, He will guide you into all truth; for He will not speak on His own authority, but whatever He hears He will speak; and He will tell you things to come. He will glorify me, for He will take of what is mine and declare it to you **(John 16:13-14)**. There are ways to extract meaning and purpose from the word of God.

Many people have carried the word of God. Some have went by

the word of God. Others have gone in the word. All of these ways have led individuals to communicate, relate, and fellowship with Christ. They are actively involved with Christ. He is supplying their breath, energy, commitment, and passion for living. Even their interests and desires come from Him.

Believers experience excitement, enthusiasm, and intense energy from being in relationship and fellowship with Christ. Jesus will exhilarate you through His word. Everyone has a strong desire to excel. Nothing is more important for success in God than a positive attitude. There should be a positive relationship between a husband and a wife. Parents should have a strong positive relationship with their children. Christ will cause these positive relationships to overflow into the church where we bring our values from home. Let's broaden our godly wisdom and knowledge for the new millennium. It will take godly wisdom and knowledge to synthesize the overflow of worldly information. Information will bewilder us in this new millennium. We will need godly minds to sift, sort, process and select information to benefit our existence.

Always, remember the Bible because it is the best-selling book of all time. This book will inform and transform men, women, boys, and girls. Transformation takes place in the inner being. Sometimes, long before any manifestation because it starts in the spirit, soul, and mind of a person.

CHAPTER 13

With Him

"He that spared not his own Son, but delivered him up for us all, how shall he not **with him** also, freely give us all things" (**Romans 8:32, emphasis added**). How can He give us all things? It's being made known in His words **with Him**. Now, I know why He says, "But seek ye first the Kingdom of God, and His righteousness; And all these things shall be added unto you" **Matthew 6:33**). All these things shall be added unto you because He freely gives us all things.

We have all these things above all things because **with Him** they come. He brings His name, authority, power, divine nature, anointing, grace, mercy, peace, rest, strength, wisdom, knowledge, and understanding to use **all these things** to acquire other things. With Him comes prosperity, healing, deliverance, and wholeness. "What shall we then say to these things? If God be for us, who can be against us?" (**Romans 8:31, KJV**).

We have access to everything that belongs to Him freely.

Cooperate with Him, and He will cooperate with you. "All things were made by Him; and without Him was not anything made that was made" (**John 1:3**). "By the word of the Lord were the heavens made; and all the host of them by the breath of His mouth" (**Psalm 33:6**).

"And to make all men see what is the fellowship of the mystery, which from the beginning of the world hath been hid in God, who created **<u>all things</u>** by Jesus Christ" (**Ephesians 3:9, emphasis added**).

"For by him were all things created that are in heaven, and that are in earth, visible and invisible, whether they be thrones, or dominions, principalities, or powers; **<u>All things</u>** were created by Him and for Him. And he is **<u>before all things,</u>** and by him all things consist" (**Colossians 1:16-17, emphasis added**).

"And **<u>God saw everything</u>** that he had made, and behold, it **<u>was very good</u>**. And the evening and the morning were the sixth day" (**Genesis 1:31, emphasis added**).

CHAPTER 14

Above All Things Divine Release

All believers will see divine release going into the 21st century. The anointing was released over two thousand years ago. Therefore, we are standing under the spout where the glory comes out because He has given us all things freely. The key is to accept God's promises with a thank you. Things are yours and mine as we receive them in prayer and not after prayers.

We must see ourselves with the things when we are praying for them in the spirit. God released His anointing in you when you received Him as your savior. He filled you up into overflowing. The overflow is to be released to someone else who has never tasted the Bread of life. The Bread of life will fill you every day. That is why we say give us our daily bread (**Matthew 6:11**).

We are receiving His divine nature when our daily Bread is His word. Also, we have a divine connection with Him. With Him, we have the Master ruling our spirits mind, body, and soul. The Master can release His will into our lives after we ask Him.

Remember He is the Master key of divine release. His divine presence is the only thing that can unlock things in the spirit and natural world because He created them with His words and spirit. That's why it's necessary to return to the original owner of everything instead of Satan who tries to copy. Our divine release comes from the greatest source Jesus Christ's blood.

CHAPTER 15

God's Presence

In the beginning God moved, God said, God saw, God divided, God called, and God made. God's move is a sharp indication of His presence because movement means motion. The bible says "And the Spirit of God moved upon the face of the waters. His Spirit is moving upon the face of the waters. How was His Spirit moving? When was it moving? What did it look like as it moved?

Isaiah 40:13 asks this question: "Who hath directed the Spirit of the Lord, or being his counselor hath taught him?" Also, verse 14 says, "with whom took the counsel and who instructed him, and taught him in the path of judgment, and taught him knowledge, and shewed to him the way of understanding?"

Scholars can question God's movements from generation to generation, but there is no way to comprehend how and when God moves. He moves in His time, space, and place. It's time for humans to recognize His internal existence because we take it too lightly. His existence is equally important both internally and externally.

Therefore, we cannot deny His presence.

His presence is evident in **John 1:1**, "in the beginning was the word, and the word was God." Then verse 2 states, "the same was in the beginning." The same God, the same Spirit, the same creative power, and the same movement of His presence. His presence is the same today. Our trends, circumstances, economics status, social status, problems, and ideals are changing constantly.

Meanwhile, God is the same source of whatever we need according to His word. His word only needs agreement to work in our lives. John writes, "If ye abide in me, and my words abide in you, ye shall ask what ye will, and it shall be done unto you." **(John 15:7, KJV)**. Here we see His abiding presence, but Christians need to be in agreement and abiding in His word that is life. Then Matthew replied, "and, lo, I am with you always, even unto the end of the world amen" **(Matthew 28:20)**. Concern yourself with what God is doing in your life because His presence is with you always.

Always though the valley, always up in the mountain, always through the tunnel, always through the pain, hurt, disappointment, and always through every circumstance. The word leads me to talk in the Spirit, which is God's presence in Holy Ghost. The Holy Ghost is the force, or power, behind creativity and existence.

"And the earth was without form, and void; and darkness was upon the face of the deep, and the Spirit, which is God's presence being the Holy Ghost. The Holy Ghost is the force, or power, behind creativity and existence.

God created us with His holy breath and for His pleasure. "And the Lord God formed man of the dust of the ground, and breathed into his nostrils the breath of life; and man became a living soul" **(Genesis 2:7)**. Man became a living soul because of the creative power and strength in God's holy breath. His breath is holy and, therefore, we have something that is powerful and precious.

Breath is a strong connection to our Creator who is the almighty God. That is why everything that has breath should praise God. Praising God leads to worship, which leads to an intimate relationship with God. Relationship with God is precious and real. Real relationships experience each other's presence. One becomes intertwined with the other. Relationships are built on knowing the other person on an intimate level. This intimate level is not feeling or lust. Rather, it is trust beyond feelings and limits.

It is unlimited yielding oneself to another being without conditions, constraints, restraints, or feelings. Then one becomes vulnerable before God in His presence to be led by Him, as a Shepherd has to be present to be followed. Therefore, we need His presence to lead and guide us through every circumstance and situation.

CHAPTER 16

Get Acquainted With God

"Acquaint now thyself with Him, and be at peace: thereby good shall come unto thee. Receive, I pray thee, the law from his mouth, and lay up His words in thine heart. If thou return to the almighty, thou shalt be built up; thou shalt put away iniquity far from thy tabernacles. Then shalt thou lay up gold as dust, and the gold of Ophir as the stones of the brooks. Yea, the Almighty shall be thy defense, and thou shalt have plenty of silver. For then shalt thou have thy delight in the Almighty, and shalt lift up thy face unto God. Thou shalt make thy prayer unto him, and he shall hear thee, and thou shalt pay thy vows. Thou shalt also decree a thing, and it shall be established unto thee: And the light shall shine upon thy ways." **(Job 22:21-28, KJV)**.

There are people the world over who are acquainted with God and they are walking in the overflow of his blessings and goodness.

The Psalmist states, "The young lions do lack, and suffer hunger, but they that seek the Lord shall not want any good thing.

(Psalm 34:10 KJV). Young lions will wonder off from the den by separating themselves from the den. There are a lot of people separated from the Lord today in sin. They can return to the Lord because He is everywhere you turn. The young lions may never find their den.

We can find Almighty God. God is not lost, but the person who sins is lost. A lost person needs to repent. Job repented by stating, wherefore, I abhor myself, and repent in dust and ashes **(Job 42:6)**. Repentance means to change completely. Also abhor means to turn away from the stench. We can turn and change like Job. Job replied, so the Lord blessed the latter end of Job more than his beginning **(Job 42:12a)**.

All believer's shout for joy because we are experiencing the latter overflow of the Holy Spirit. He saved the best for last. That's why the writer of Acts stated, "And it shall come to pass in the last days, saith God, I will pour out of my spirit upon all flesh" **(Acts 2:17a)**. We have a spirit powered church today. Believers have stepped into a power-saturated gospel. The gospel provides spirit and blood covering against Satan today. Satan flees because he can't stand the blood covering of Jesus. Also, the blood, spirit, and word is above all things in the life of a believer.

CHAPTER 17

Reserved Released Power

"And when Jesus had cried with a loud voice, he said, Father, into thy hands I commend my Spirit; and having said this he gave up the Ghost" **(Luke 23:46)**. That's why Jesus didn't fight back, nor complain. He was giving power for our last days.

Now, Jesus knows Satan is defeated. We should know this today. Stop looking for Jesus in emptiness.

"And they found the stone rolled away from the sepulcher. And they entered in and found not the body of the Lord Jesus" **(Luke 24:2-3)**. They were looking for Jesus in the wrong place. Stop looking for Jesus in old dead religious, doctrines of men, and hollow places.

"He is not here, but is risen; remember how he spake unto you when he was yet in Galilee. Saying. The Son of man must be delivered unto the hands of sinful men, and be crucified, and the third day rise again. And they remembered his words" **(Luke 24:25-26)**.

"Then he said unto them, O fools, and slow heart to believe all that the prophets have spoken" (**Luke 24:25**).

"And hath raised us up together, and made us sit together in heavenly places in Christ Jesus" (**Ephesians 2:6**).

If ye then were raised with Christ, seek those things that are above, where Christ sitteth on the right hand of God. Set your affection on things above, not on things on earth. (**Colossians 3:1,2**). God's power is released throughout the world today. Believers are being enhanced throughout the world.

This power released has substance because it is flowing in the Word of God. God is the word, power, and strength that contains substance. The spoken word is above all things.

"For the Lord is good and his mercy is everlasting and His truth endureth to all generations" (**Psalm 100:5**). His truth performs above all truth. Also, His truth will and is still performing **above all things**.

No one can stop this released power. God's power has caused effective working relationships in the body of Christ. His power promotes collaboration and cooperation among believers. Believers are working together for the best interest of the body of Christ. The working relationship is a result of this tremendous source of energy and power provided through the Holy Ghost. Positive working relationships serve as emotional support in the body of Christ.

Throughout the body of Christ, resources are increasing. Church members and ministers are rallying behind one another to improve involvement in the local assembly. The Holy Ghost concentrates on providing directions. Also, He concerns Himself with communication and motivation. God's power is released to get us more actively involved in our communities.

Our communities need leaders who will confront new challenges. God's power will enhance our ability to succeed in the twenty first century. We must come into agreement with the Holy Ghost to supply the twenty first century with leaders. Leadership through almighty God will posses stability and quality of life.

Believe, since "we have the same spirit of faith according to what is written, I believed and therefore I spoken, we also believe and speak. Knowing that He who raised up the Lord Jesus will also raise us up with Jesus and will present us with you. For all things are for your sakes, that grace, having spread through the many, may cause thanksgiving to abound to the Glory of God." **(II Corinthians 4:13-15, NKJV)**.

Most Christians believe and receive our heavenly position down here on earth! By faith, we are covered with the blood of Jesus when we stand before the throne of God. God only sees the blood of Jesus and not our sins. God sees our gift of righteousness as believers through Jesus Christ because the blood covers us when we stand before God. The Bible states, but now the righteousness of God without the law is manifested, being witnessed by the law and prophets, even the righteousness of God which is by faith of Jesus Christ unto **all** and upon all them that believer: For there is no difference; **(Romans 3:21-22, KJV)**. Another scripture verifies our gift of righteousness. That scripture says, "For He hath made him to be sin for us, who knew no sin; that **we might be made the righteousness of God in Him**." Knowing we have the gift of righteousness appropriate the word in our lives.

CHAPTER 18

All Things Are Possible

"And Mary said, Behold the handmaid of the Lord; be it unto me according to thy word. And the angel departed from her" (**Luke 1:38**).

"And all things, whatsoever ye shall ask in prayer, believing, ye shall receive" (**Matthew 21:22**).

First, there is nothing impossible with God. That is why it's important to cooperate with God. Be it unto me according to Thy word. Not popular opinion, or feelings, but according to Thy word. Thy word will manifest all things, whatever I pray for according to God's will. God's word is His will. Every genuine principle for succeeding is found in the word of God.

Believe and receive from God because He said it, not you. We must conceive the word of God, as Mary, regardless of who we are in life.

Receiving the Word will change our circumstances. When Mary received the word, it changed the world. Receiving the Word of

God gives us the ability, strength, and power to change things around us. Believers need to speak God's word until their circumstances change. Be convinced that God's Word works.

Work the Word in your life now. As a child of God, learn to trust God. We have what God says we have. We will be healed, because we are healed. We must change our thinking. Thoughts such as "God put this pain and suffering on me: are not true. God came that we might have life. He did not come to hurt or harm us in anyway. In retrospect, organized religion has put these thoughts in our head.

The only way believers suffer is for the word of God. When we confess the word of God, most of our oppositions come from religious folks who do not believe the word of God. It is shocking to believe God for something, while your brothers and sisters doubt it. That tells us, we are not worshipping the same God. People who are part of the true church want to see other believers succeed. Believers are praying for the advancement and prosperity of the church.

The church will advance and prosper because it is founded upon Jesus Christ whose the Advancer. "And all things, whatsoever ye shall ask in prayer, believing, ye shall receive" **(Matthew 21:22).**

"And this is the confidence that we have in Him, that if we ask anything according to his will, He heareth us. And if we know that He hears us, whatsoever we ask, we know that we have the petitions that we desired of Him" **(I John 5:14-15, KJV).** God placed a desire in me to be wealthy when I was in the fourth grade. God has placed 35,000 members in my heart for First Christian Church in Stuart, Virginia. That is one of the desires from God, but there are many more for Stuart, Virginia.

The human mind would not be able to understand what is in my heart for Stuart, Virginia, but God can because I know He hears me. But His Word states, "therefore I say unto you, what things so ever ye desire, when ye pray, believe that ye receive them, and ye shall have them" (**Mark 11:22**). There will be more people in his new millennium walking in the faith of fire of God.

There is a new 21st century believer. The 21st century believer believes that God is a dead raiser, and healer, and a deliverer. We are walking by faith and not by sight. Trust levels have risen, and we are walking in a level above all things. This generation is tired of dead religion. Young people are tired of not seeing a move of God. Wherever Jesus is, there is a move of God.

"And when he was come unto Jerusalem, all the city was moved, saying, who is this?" (**Matthew 21:10**). Jesus moves the moneychanger. Jesus moves the chief priest and scribes. Jesus moves the little children. Jesus will move you with joy, happiness, health, wealth, deliverance, and praise. On the other hand, Satan will move you with doubt, envy, strife, fear, and jealousy of what Jesus is doing. Jesus' move is so powerful until little children began to praise Him.

"And when the Chief Priests and scribes saw the wonderful things that he did, and the children crying in the temple, and saying. Hosanna to the Son of David; they were so displeased, and said unto him Hearest thou what these say? And Jesus saith unto them yea. Have ye never read, "out of the mouth of babes and sucklings thou hast perfected praise?" **(Matthew 21:15-16)**.

Religious leaders wanted to stop the children from praising God. Jesus kindly rebukes them with the word of God. Praising God is a command today. Praises of God are reigning out from seashore to seashore.

"I was glad when they said unto me, let us go into the house of the Lord" **(Psalm 122:1)**. People are glad to be in the house of God. They are not watching the clock or looking for ways to get out of the service of the Lord. They are running to God with energy to fulfill His commission.

"Praise ye the Lord, sing unto the Lord a new song, and his praise in the congregations of saints" **(Psalm 149:1)**.

"Let everything that hath breath praise the Lord, praise ye the Lord" **(Psalm 150:6)**.

"One generation shall praise thy works to another, and shall declare thy mighty acts" **(Psalm 145:4)**.

CHAPTER 19

Blessed

◆━━◉◯━━◆

"**B**lessed shalt thou be when thou comest in, and blessed shalt thou be when thou goest out" (**Deuteronomy 28:6**).

"The Lord bless thee, and keep thee. The Lord make his face shine upon thee. The Lord lift up his countenance upon thee, and give the peace" (**Numbers 6:24-26**).

"And I will make thee a great nation, and I will bless thee, and make thy name great; and thou shalt be a blessing" (**Genesis 12:2**).

Blessed to be a blessing. That is why Luke tells us, "give, and it shall be given unto you; good measure, pressed down, and shaken together, and running over, shall men give unto your bosom. For with the same measure that ye mete withal it shall be measured to you again" (**Luke 6:38**). We are marked to be blessed by the Best.

"The blessings of the Lord, it maketh rich, and he addeth no sorrow with it" (**Proverbs 10:2**).

"Riches and honor are with me; yea, durable riches and righteousness" (**Proverbs 8:18**).

You are the children of the prophets, and of the covenant, which God made with our fathers, saying unto Abraham, "and in thy seed shall all the kindreds of the earth be blessed." It was agreed upon in the Old and New Testaments that we are blessed upon the word of God. God's word is truth to be performed in our lives today. His word is producing throughout the body of Christ.

Do you realize God's word has to perform if you believe it and receive it? Why? Because God swore by Himself. He cannot lie.

"For all the promises of God in him are yea, and in him Amen, unto the glory of God by us. Now he which stablished us with you in Christ, and hath anointed us, is God; who hath also sealed us, and given the earnest of the spirit of our hearts. Moreover, I call God for a record upon my soul, that to spare you I came not as yet unto Corinth. Not for that we have dominion over your faith, but are helpers of your joy; for by faith ye stand" **(2 Corinthians 1:20-24).**

God has already blessed us through His yes and Amen. Also, by faith we are sealed in that blessing. Jesus signed it into being with His blood. Faith makes it real in the life of a believer. By faith, we stand in the blessings of the Lord. No one or nothing can move a believer out of his position. Church, position yourself for the greater blessings in this new millennium.

"Beloved, I wish above all things that thou mayest prosper and be in health, even as thy soul prospereth" **(3 John 2)**. John is sharing this with us because he knew the supernatural power of God toward His church. It's for us today if we will only believe and receive it now.

"Now, when he had left speaking, he said unto Simon, launch out into the deep, and let down your nets for a drought. And Simon answering said unto him. Master, we have toiled all the night, and have taken nothing; nevertheless at thy word I will let down the net" **(Luke 5:4-5)**. Peter was saying I obey your word above all things. Even though, my profession is fishing and I have fished here many times, but I have experienced Jesus. I will respond to Your word above all things.

Look what happened when he obeyed Jesus who was the word. The word will put supernatural abundance in our lives. Act now on the word of God. Don't let ignorance, pride, intellect, experience, and independence stand in the way of God's word. "And when they had this done, they enclosed a great multitude of fishes; and their net broke." Doing it Jesus' way is the only way.

"Jesus saith unto him, I am the way, the truth, and the life. No man cometh unto the father, but by me" **(John 14:6)**. Above all things, "trust in the Lord with all thine heart; and lean not unto thine own understanding in all thy ways acknowledge him, and he shall direct thy paths" **(Proverbs 3:5-6)**. Almighty God is the director of our lives above all things. The body of Christ is a symphony and God is the Director.

We all play our unique part in the body of Christ. Our unity, harmony, sound, and uniformity is best heard and seen when He directs. His Bride is a major symphony here on earth. His Bride is not cheap, nor misplaced. This symphony only plays to His direction. Everyone knows his part by carefully paying attention to the Director.

The Director's tune is good news. There is good news in the world today. Therefore, play your part in the 21st century. Don't try to play someone else's part. Your instrument is needed. All of us can be a part of this symphony regardless of race, creed, color, social, economic, and political status.

Above all thins, you can be part of the top rank and file. Maybe, you were not a great athlete, musician, movie star, or business owner. However, you can sit in heavenly places with Jesus Christ while you are still on this earth. You can be an instrument used by the almighty God to prosper and advance the kingdom of God on earth as it is in heaven. The kingdom of God has launched an all out offensive against the kingdom of darkness.

CHAPTER 20

Offensive Against Darkness

We have been trained by the word of God, the Holy Ghost, and the Father.

"For the weapons of our warfare are not carnal, but mighty through God to the pulling down of strongholds" (**2 Corinthians 10:4**). The body of Christ has launched one of the biggest air assaults against the powers of darkness in the history of all times.

All the frontline troops have been waiting to move into the things of God. People have prayed us into this position. Position yourself to march into enemy held territory. The territory is now yours because of the anointing of the Holy Ghost. Go in and take everything that belongs to you and God.

"No weapon that is formed against thee shall proper; and every tongue that shall rise against thee in judgment thou shalt condemn. This is the heritage of the servants of the Lord, and their righteousness is of me, saith the Lord" (**Isaiah 54:17**).

Our offensive is driven by the armor of God. We are covered by

God's armor to advance the kingdom. We have some people who have been uniquely trained to handle anything the enemy throws at them. They can go into a situation with God's armor on and build from their training. They know how to move in the spirit of "as it is written." They know where the power of God operates and how it operates. Believers are on the move and they can't be stopped. Why? "And I say also unto thee, that thou art Peter, and upon this rock I will build my church; and the gates of hell shall not prevail against it" **(Matthew 4:4)**. We win because we are part of a prevailing church. Remember, **above all things** as it is written. "Man shall not live by bread alone, but by every word that proceedeth out of the mouth of God" **(Deuteronomy 8:3)**. Believers are operating in what God says.

CHAPTER 21

Propelled

The body of Christ is being propelled into awesomeness. The fuel is the power of the Holy Ghost. We are talking about supersonic moves of God's spirit. God has already done some things that are baffling to all of us in Christ. We see mega-churches today. We have people reaching millions by television and radio. We have the Internet. Expect the following in the future for the body of Christ:

- More money
- More mega-churches
- Many more souls
- 'Many healings
- More planes for ministers
- More luxury transportation
- More buses
- More paid staff

God is going to supply our ministers for His glory. He loves to glorify His body. He is changing us from glory to glory. Next, we are prepared to strike anywhere in the world. God has prepared us to strike with the fire of the Holy Ghost. God has some people whom you have never heard of on stand by. The second He says move, we are ready, anointed to operate in the gift's of the Spirit.

"Every good gift and every perfect gift is from above, and cometh down from the father of lights, with whom is no variableness, neither show of turning" (**James 1:17**).

"For God hath not given us the spirit of fear; but of power, and of love, and of a sound mind' (**2 Timothy 1:7**). God has placed some people out here who are not afraid because they love you enough to call sin, sin and not compromise. Also, they have enough power to call sin out of a sinner. Believers are clear thinkers. That is why they have a sound mind. "Finally, my brethren, be strong in the Lord, and in the power of his might" (**Ephesians 6:10**).

CHAPTER 22

A Fire Influenced Destiny

"And the Angel of the Lord appeared unto him in a flame of fire out of the midst of a bush; and he looked, and, behold, the bush burned with fire, and the bush was not consumed" **(Exodus 3:2)**.

God brings fire into believers' lives to excel their destiny. Moses was accompanied by fire throughout His journey into the Promise Land.

"And the Lord went before them by day in a pillar of a cloud, to lead them the way; and by night in a pillar of fire, to give them light, to go by day and night" **(Exodus 13:21)**.

"For the cloud of the Lord was upon the tabernacle by day, and fire was on it by night, in the sight of all the house of Israel, throughout all their journey" **(Exodus 40:48)**. Fire is provided to us throughout our Christian journey.

"I indeed baptize you with water unto repentance; but he that cometh after me is mightier than I, whose shoes I am not worthy to bear, he shall baptize you with the Holy Ghost and with fire" **(Matthew 3:11)**.

Fire is provided in the New Testament to believers to consume and influence darkness to become light. [THIS FIRE WILL PURGE ALL THE DARKNESS AND SIN OUT OF OUR LIVES?] The fire of God will consume everything in our path. God's fire in us will call attention to our life. Also, this fire will attract others to come to Christ. This fire is the lift off power we need to leave here during the rapture. Meanwhile, we are to walk by God's fire, warming the hearts of the cold and oppressed.

Others will model our fire. Therefore, others cannot influence us. This fire is eternal and will not go out. Jesus Christ our High Priest made this fire. Our fire can't be put out by anyone. This fire represents the angel of God. Our journey will be complete and powerful. Securing our predestined destiny, Christ has positioned us as a burning torch above all things. Christ has to fulfill His promises and the fire in us to honor His truth. We are God's church, His bride, and bright and morning star. No one can stop God through Jesus Christ from perfecting His destined church. That is enough assurance to take us from earth to Glory. We are being changed from glory to glory.

"For therein is the righteousness of God, being revealed from faith to faith, as it is written the just shall live by faith" **(Romans 1:17)**. Keep the faith, only to deposit into your situation through the word of God. God has to bless you through His word.

CHAPTER 23

The Kingdom of God Seizes Darkness

"To open their eyes, in order to turn them from darkness to light, and from the power of Satan to God, that they may receive forgiveness of sins and an inheritance among those who are sanctified by faith in me" (**Acts 26:18**).

The kingdom of God has enough power to seize everything in His path. The kingdom brings the King into existence. Wherever the King of kings is everything has to flee. The King comes with His blood, word, authority, angels, and spirit to occupy one enemy-held territory. Now, the kingdom belongs to the children of Light.

"Yet in all these things we are more than conquerors through Him who loved us" (**Romans 8:37**). Christ has done the work by being the conqueror. Therefore, we are more than conquerors who have acquired increase beyond the conqueror. God escalated us into the position of the Blessed in this new millennium.

Therefore, let no one boast in men. For **all things are yours**. "Whether Paul or Apollos or Cephas, or the world or life or death, or thing present or things to come **all are yours**" (**1 Corinthians 3:21-22, emphasis added**). Above all things, believers are more than sickness, lack, disease, drugs, alcohol, prostitution, poverty, and man-made doctrines.

CHAPTER 24

To Equipped to Get Whipped

⊷⟺⟺⊶

All born-again believers wear the whole armor of God from head to toe—from the helmet of salvation to our feet being shod with the preparation of the gospel. Always use God's equipment because it works; satisfaction guaranteed. It repels demons because it was purchased with the blood of Jesus. The new 21st century believers will not back up, but they will go forward. Believers realize the price Christ paid for us to move into the things of God.

Well functioning Christians will efficiently and effectively appropriate the word of God where there is scarcity. They will do so in a number of different ways. First, Christians have an interest to work hard to produce new Christians and godly leaders because, these new godly men and women will gain an advantage over darkness in the world. Also, these leaders react to the shortage of good leaders.

The kingdom of God has a responsibility to provide positive

benefits, such as: protection, safety, purpose, plans, quality, interest and support for believers. New Christian leaders are exceeding their previous leaders. No disrespect, our previous leaders did what they knew to do. However, leaders in this 21st century are benefiting from the word of God above all things.

They are operating in the performance of the word of God. God is demonstrating His power and authority through these new leaders in a magnificent way. God is being exalted above all things through these new leaders. The word of God is constructing lives so rapidly today. People are reacting and responding all over the world to the word of God. Sometimes it's positive and sometimes it's negative. Meanwhile, God has an expected end, regardless of our positive or negative attitude. We cannot undermine God's word because it is going to stand above all things. Therefore, let us accept it with a simple thank you.

CHAPTER 25

Relevant Leaders

People are looking for leaders—preachers and teachers—who keep the word of God relevant, instead of giving many interpretations. Most people realize a need for a relevant word from God. Then God's word is received with clarity and favorable confidence in its ability to perform in any situation.

Giving a careful relevant word in churches will enhance support and performance among members in the 21st century. Behavior in our churches will be defined or related to the relevant word of God above all things. A relevant word from God will inspire loyalty and enthusiasm in the body of Christ. Also, the body of Christ will establish and maintain a strong power base throughout the world, based on the word of God above all things.

The word of God is transforming traditional churches into Holy Ghost environments, instead of just a "so-so" church. People are being transformed into greater leaders inside and outside the church.

"And do not be conformed to this world, but be transformed by the renewing of your mind, that you may prove what is good and acceptable and perfect will of God" **Romans 12:2**). Believers who are transformed will take a relevant word outside the church to sinners.

Sinners are looking for a relevant word instead of all these man-made doctrines, religions, and traditions. People want the gospel and not gossip. The perfect will of God is above all things. It is necessary to spend a lot of time importing a relevant word in our communities. Leaders are overcoming fear, doubt, and unbelief by becoming obedient to God's word above all things.

Obedience means going against status quo, family, friends, and some other beliefs.

People will not like you in the beginning because of their status quo mentality. Contrary, you must step out into the things of God. God has already handed you His mantle. He has given the Holy Ghost to you. Now, can he get it through you to someone else? Then God said, "Let us make man in our image according to our likeness" **Genesis 1:26a**).

God will not be defeated because He is determined to make us in His likeness. I don't care how bad your sin is; God loves you and not the sin. That is why God raised up judges, prophets, priest, Jesus, evangelist, apostles, teachers, and pastors to deposit His likeness into our being. "But we all, with unveiled face, beholding as in a mirror the glory of the Lord, are <u>**being transformed into the same image from**</u> glory to glory. Just as by the spirit of the Lord" **(2 Corinthians 3:18, emphasis added)**.

The mirror of a relevant word will transform us into His image. Like things attract one another. Our image is His image. God's image is so powerfully radiated through the Holy Ghost. The Holy Ghost is the ingredient that transforms us into His image. The word above all things is the stuff for the puff. When something is blown upon, it will puff up.

The body of Christ is so full until it is time to overflow into our communities. "He that believeth on me as the scripture saith, out of his belly shall flow rivers of living water" **(John 7:38)**. God likeness and life is flowing into everyone who receives Him.

"Being confident of this very thing, that he who has begun a good work in you will complete it until the day of Jesus Christ" **(Philippians 1:7)**.

Therefore, we need to work out what God has worked in us as believers. Above all things work it out into our communities. God didn't perform in us to lay idle. There is too much power, joy, peace, wisdom, knowledge, and understanding inside of us being misused competing and arguing about who has it. Real believers are about their Father's business above all things. They do not waste time with the above-mentioned people. The advancement of the kingdom of God is their first priority.

God has given us a vast area to spread the gospel. Therefore, it will take every waking hour to seize darkness to advance the kingdom. Take charge of your region through the power of the almighty God through Jesus Christ in prayer. The results are overwhelming because revival is advancing in these regions. To God be all the glory.

CHAPTER 26

Rich Above All Things

"For you know the grace of our Lord Jesus Christ, that though he was rich, yet for your sakes, He became poor, that you through His poverty might become rich" **(2 Corinthians 8:9)**. How can we be poor if He became poor for us to become rich? Every believer's testimony should be, I am rich through Jesus Christ. Again, religion, tradition, opinions, and man-made doctrines have helped keep people poor.

Believers are accepting the truth above all things because they belong to a blessed church. That is the true living church of God. Now may He who supplies seed to the sower, and bread for food, supply and multiply the seed you have sown and increase the fruits of your righteousness. While you are **enriched in everything** for all liberality, which causes thanksgiving through us to God. Thank God above all things.